FAMOUS PEO

Biographies of famous people to
support the curriculum.

John Logie
Baird

by Nicola Baxter
Illustrations by Richard Morgan

W
FRANKLIN WATTS
LONDON•SYDNEY

First published in 2000
by Franklin Watts
This edition 2002

Franklin Watts
96 Leonard Street
London EC2A 4XD

Franklin Watts Australia
56 O'Riordan Street
Alexandria, Sydney
NSW 2015

ISBN 0 7496 4342 0 (pbk)

A CIP catalogue record for this book is
available from the British Library

Dewey Decimal Classification
Number: 621.388

Editor: Louise John

Printed in Great Britain

John Logie Baird

Just over one hundred years ago, in 1888, John Logie Baird was born. His parents, the Reverend John and his wife Jessie, already had two daughters and a son. They all lived on the west coast of Scotland.

3

Although he was never very healthy, young John had a lively mind. He soon became interested in science – especially anything to do with electricity.

In those days, very few people had electric lights or telephones in their homes. John read about any new inventions and was soon trying out ideas himself.

John! What are you doing?

When he was a boy, John set up
his own telephone exchange in
his bedroom. He rigged up lines
across the street to the homes
of four of his friends. It worked
really well.

But, one night, a storm brought one of the lines down. The driver of a horse-drawn cab was flung from his seat as he drove by. He complained to the official telephone company. They soon discovered John's system – and closed it down!

Next, John set up a generator to supply the house with electric light. The generator was made out of all kinds of bits and pieces, including old jam jars.

He also became very interested in photography. One of his experiments was to enlarge photographs, which were only black and white then. He also worked out a way to delay a picture being taken.

John was so interested in his experiments that he never seemed to notice what he was wearing or how he looked.

After leaving school, he went to the Royal Glasgow College of Technology. Meanwhile he continued his own experiments in the kitchen at home!

It was around this time that John first started thinking about the idea of television. He thought that if sounds could be sent by radio waves, then pictures could, too. For most people this was just a dream.

11

John's time at college was cut short when the First World War started in 1914. He volunteered at once to fight for his country, but he was turned down because of his poor health.

Instead, John became an engineer with the company that supplied electrical power to the shipbuilding yards and factories in Glasgow.

It was important work for the war effort, but it meant going out at any time of the day or night to fix problems. John's health began to get worse.

There must be a better way to make a living!

After the war, John decided to go into business for himself. He had quite a talent for selling his ideas and inventions.

14

Unfortunately, although the business was a success, John became ill again from working too hard. His doctor was firm with him.

John decided to go to Trinidad in the West Indies. He soon felt better, but he was bored with nothing to do so he decided to start another business. The island had plenty of fruit and sugar. Surely a jam factory would be a good idea?

Unfortunately, the jam attracted a lot of insects too and, on top of everything else, John caught malaria. Perhaps a hot climate wasn't so healthy after all.

Back in London, John stayed with his sister for a while. He wondered about working as a scientist again, and asked her advice on what he should do.

But after a few more business ventures, John became very seriously ill. He was sent to Hastings on the south coast of England to get better. Although he was only thirty-four, John felt as though his life was over.

Very, very slowly, his health improved. After a few months, John found he needed something to occupy his mind again. As he could not take on a job, he thought about science once more.

It's years since I studied. There are so many new ideas to catch up on.

John was determined to make his boyhood dream of television come true. In a small attic room, with no one to help him and no proper equipment, John set to work.

John knew that the science behind television was really quite simple. He needed to break a picture into small pieces of information, send that information as radio waves, and put the bits back together at the other end.

A German man called Paul Nipkow had already invented a revolving disk that could help with the first part. It could turn patterns of light and dark into electrical impulses that could be sent as radio signals. Another Nipkow disk would turn them back into a picture again.

In 1924, John managed to send a picture of a cross to a screen across the room. Success at last!

John's first pictures were tiny
and blurred, but he knew he
could make them better. Back in
London he had a piece of luck.
Gordon Selfridge, a wealthy
businessman, paid John to show
his invention to the public.

The demonstrations caused
a lot of excitement, but most
people did not understand
how the equipment worked.
They thought that the
machinery could somehow
'see' through solid walls!

25

John worked hard on his invention but he soon ran out of money. Even though he was having such success, it seemed that his experiments must stop.

Just in time, his Scottish relatives sent him some money. Plunging on, John made a breakthrough: he sent a picture of a ventriloquist's dummy to another room. This time it was much clearer ... he could see the nose, eyes and eyebrows!

Thrilled, the inventor rushed out to find someone to be the first person to appear on television.

27

A few minutes later, a young office boy found himself sitting in front of some enormous electric lamps. They were very, very hot. But John paid young William to sit still.

Next door, John shouted to William to turn his head and open and shut his mouth. To his delight, he could see the boy do just that on the screen in front of him!

Now it was time to show his invention to other people. On 27th January 1926, John demonstrated his television to over fifty scientists. They crowded into his tiny rooms, a few at a time.

News of John's success spread far and wide. Many people were now willing to lend him money. For the first time, John could employ people to help him in his work.

In 1927, he used two telephone
lines to transmit television from
London to Glasgow. One
carried the pictures and the
other the sound.

Less than a year later, television pictures were sent from London to New York. Soon after that passengers on a boat in the Atlantic Ocean saw friends and relatives in London on a television screen.

In 1929, the British Broadcasting Corporation (BBC), which had been set up in 1922 for radio broadcasts, began transmitting its first television programmes.

A 'Televisor', as John called it, was even set up for the Prime Minister. There were three programmes a week, each lasting only fifteen minutes!

Before long, more programmes were being broadcast. They were all 'live'. People watching their 'Televisor' at home saw performances that were going on at that very moment. Singers, dancers and actors had to get it right first time ...

Television went from strength to strength. The first outside broadcasts showed famous sporting events. In cinemas, television was shown on the large screen.

Although the 'Televisors' were expensive, more and more people were buying them. Only the BBC was broadcasting, so there was no quarrelling about which channel to watch! And, of course, all the programmes were in black and white.

John was enjoying success at last. His health improved, his money worries were behind him and he was admired wherever he went.

In 1931, he travelled to America, where he was greeted as a genius. While he was there, he met and married Margaret Albu, a concert pianist.

But success did not stop John working. He constantly looked for improvements to his system, as well as developing new ideas for other inventions.

39

In fact, John's system was not in use for very long. In 1937, the BBC chose a rival system that used a completely different method of scanning pictures. It was a blow to John, but did not stop him working on other ideas.

John helped to invent lots of things. His 'Noctovision', for example, used infra-red rays to 'see' in the dark. Today, the police, firefighters and soldiers all rely on infra-red cameras and goggles in their jobs.

Please find me.

John's ideas were also used in the development of Radar, which is used to help ships and aircraft find their way. Fax machines and video recorders also might not be here today without his work.

A computer mouse sends
signals to its computer by
shining light through slots
in turning wheels. It's an idea
that John helped to develop over
seventy years ago.

John Logie Baird died in 1946. He was only fifty-seven, but he had achieved an enormous amount in his life. In 1931, he talked on the radio about his hope that the home 'Televisor' would soon become as common as the home radio.

He was right, even though we have a different name for it. Today, television is so much part of our lives that it is hard to imagine doing without it.

What's more, television is developing all the time – just as John Logie Baird would have wished!

Further facts

Black-and-white pictures

To make sure that the final picture was as clear as possible, singers, dancers and presenters on early black-and-white television had to wear special make-up. That meant dead white faces, blue lipstick and blue eyeshadow!

Deceiving the eye

Television screens, like cinema ones, don't really show us moving pictures. What we see are still pictures, each slightly different from the last, flashing in front of our eyes many times a second. At this speed, our brains don't have time to make sense of each picture, so they merge together and seem to be moving.

Some important dates in John Logie Baird's lifetime

1888 John Logie Baird is born in Helensburgh, Scotland.

1914 John's education is interrupted by the beginning of the First World War.

1922 John goes to Hastings on the south coast of England to recover from illness. There he starts experimenting with television.

1926 John makes the first successful public demonstration of real television.

1929 The British Broadcasting Corporation (BBC) starts transmitting television programmes using John's system.

1931 John travels to America, where he marries.

1946 John Logie Baird dies aged 57.